LIGUE 1

BY ASHLEY GISH

SOCCER LEAGUES

TORQUE™

BELLWETHER MEDIA · MINNEAPOLIS, MN

Torque brims with excitement perfect for thrill-seekers of all kinds. Discover daring survival skills, explore uncharted worlds, and marvel at mighty engines and extreme sports. In *Torque* books, anything can happen. Are you ready?

This edition first published in 2025 by Bellwether Media, Inc.

Library of Congress Cataloging-in-Publication Data

LC record for Ligue 1 available at: https://lccn.loc.gov/2024022429

Editor: Kieran Downs Designer: Gabriel Hilger

Printed in the United States of America, North Mankato, MN.

TABLE OF CONTENTS

THE CLASSIC

It is an exciting 2024 Ligue 1 match between **rivals** Paris Saint-Germain (PSG) and Olympique de Marseille. The score is tied 0–0.

PSG takes the ball up the middle of the field. They pass the ball outside. Then they pass back to the middle. They score! Late in the match, PSG scores again. They hold on to win 2–0!

PARIS SAINT-GERMAIN

TOP TEAMS

Matches between Marseille and PSG are called *Le Classique*, which means "The Classic."

WHAT IS LIGUE 1?

Ligue 1 is the top soccer league in France and Monaco. There are 18 teams in the league. Fans get excited about their favorite teams.

Ligue 1 teams are known for training young players. These players often become some of the best in the world. The league is also known for the **strategies** that its coaches come up with.

HISTORY OF LIGUE 1

Soccer became popular in France during the early 1900s. France's national team began playing in **tournaments**. But the country did not have any **professional** leagues.

In 1932, the first professional league formed. It was called National. There were 20 teams in the league. In 1933, the league changed its name to Division 1.

1904 FRENCH NATIONAL TEAM

ALL TIED UP

France's national team played its first match in 1904. The match ended in a tie against Belgium.

FOUNDING TEAMS

- ANTIBES
- CA PARIS
- CANNES
- CLUB FRANÇAIS
- EXCELSIOR AC
- FC SÈTE
- HYÈRES FC
- MARSEILLE
- METZ
- MONTPELLIER
- MULHOUSE
- NICE
- OLYMPIQUE ALÈS
- OLYMPIQUE LILLOIS
- RACING CLUB DE FRANCE
- RED STAR
- RENNES
- SC FIVES
- SC NÎMES
- SOCHAUX

In 1933, Division 2 was formed. This is the second-highest level of French soccer.

In 1995, the point system changed. Teams began receiving three points instead of two for each match they won. In 2002, Division 1 and Division 2 were renamed Ligue 1 and Ligue 2. After the 2022–2023 season, Ligue 1 went down to 18 teams.

2002 LIGUE 1 MATCH

TIMELINE

1932

National has its first season

1933

National changes its name to Division 1

1995

Wins are awarded three points instead of two

2023 LIGUE 1 MATCH

WINNING STREAK

Nice was the first Division 1 team to win two Division 1 trophies in a row. They won in the 1950–1951 and 1951–1952 seasons.

2002

Division 1 is renamed Ligue 1

2023

Ligue 1 changes to have 18 teams

LIGUE 1 TODAY

The Ligue 1 season goes from August until May the following year. Each team plays against each other twice. There are 34 matches during each season.

HERE AND THERE

Each Ligue 1 team plays every other team once at their home field and once on the other team's field.

Teams are awarded three points for wins. They earn one point for ties. Zero points are awarded for losses. The team with the most points at the end of the season is the **champion**.

Teams are **promoted** and **relegated** at the end of the season. The two teams with the lowest points in Ligue 1 are relegated to Ligue 2. The two top teams in Ligue 2 are promoted to Ligue 1.

The third-place Ligue 2 team plays two **playoff** matches against the third-lowest Ligue 1 team. The team with more **goals** over both matches is promoted.

2024 LIGUE 2 MATCH

RELEGATION AND PROMOTION

1. RELEGATION

The bottom two Ligue 1 teams are relegated.

2. PROMOTION

The top two Ligue 2 teams are promoted.

3. PLAYOFFS

The third-place Ligue 2 team plays a playoff against the third-lowest Ligue 1 team. The winner plays in Ligue 1.

2024 CHAMPIONS LEAGUE MATCH

The top four teams at the end of the Ligue 1 season get to play in the **Champions League**. They play against teams from other top European leagues.

Ligue 1 teams also play in the **Coupe de France**. This tournament decides the best team in France. Ligue 1 teams play against teams from lower-level French leagues.

2023 COUPE DE FRANCE MATCH

Soccer is the number one sport in France. Fans celebrate wins with parades. They wave flags. Buildings may be lit with the winning team's colors.

Teams may have strong rivalries. PSG and Marseille are big rivals. Stadiums always fill when these two teams play. Every Ligue 1 match promises excitement!

TOP PLAYERS

RAYMOND KOPA

9

FORWARD

Played for Reims, 1951–1956, 1959–1967

DELIO ONNIS

9

FORWARD

Played for Monaco, 1973–1980

JEAN-PIERRE PAPIN

9

FORWARD

Played for Marseille, 1986–1992

ZINEDINE ZIDANE

7

MIDFIELDER

Played for Bordeaux, 1992–1996

KYLIAN MBAPPÉ

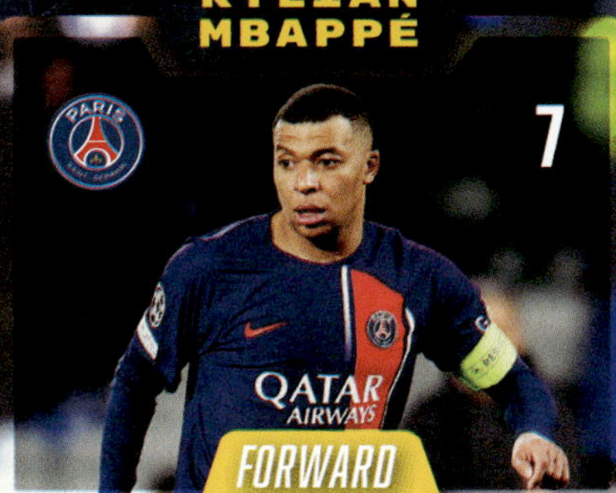

7

FORWARD

Played for Paris Saint-Germain, 2017–2024

FAST FACTS

NUMBER OF TEAMS	18
YEAR STARTED	1932

LIGUE 1
Uber Eats

LARGEST STADIUM

ORANGE VÉLODROME

MARSEILLE

Capacity: 67,394 people
Location: Marseille, France

CLUB RECORDS
(AS OF 2023)

CLUB WITH MOST APPEARANCES *MARSEILLE*	73 seasons
CLUB WITH MOST CHAMPIONSHIPS *PARIS SAINT-GERMAIN*	11
FIRST CHAMPION *OLYMPIQUE LILLOIS*	
CLUBS THAT HAVE PARTICIPATED IN THE LEAGUE	74

INDIVIDUAL RECORDS
(AS OF 2023)

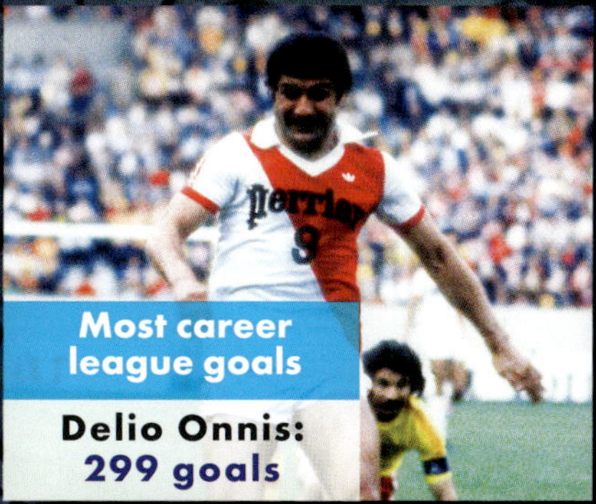

Most career league goals

Delio Onnis: 299 goals

Most goals scored in a single season

Josip Skoblar: 44 goals

Fastest goal scored

Kylian Mbappé: 8 seconds

Person with most league appearances

Mickaël Landreau: 617 appearances

GLOSSARY

champion—the winner of a contest that decides the best team or person

Champions League—a European soccer tournament where the top teams in the top European leagues play each other to decide the best team in Europe

Coupe de France—the championship tournament for professional soccer in France

goals—scores in soccer; a player scores goals by sending the ball into the other team's net.

playoff—related to matches played after the regular season is over; playoff matches decide which teams play in Ligue 1 the following year.

professional—related to a player or team that makes money playing a sport

promoted—moved up to a higher league

relegated—moved down to a lower league

rivals—long-standing opponents that compete for the same thing

strategies—actions done to win a match

tournaments—series of matches in which several teams try to win championships

TO LEARN MORE

AT THE LIBRARY

Ballheimer, David. *Soccer Legends 2024*. London, U.K.: Welbeck Publishing Group Limited, 2023.

Hornby, Hugh. *Soccer*. New York, N.Y.: DK Publishing, 2023.

McDougall, Chrös. *Soccer*. Minneapolis, Minn.: ABDO, 2023.

ON THE WEB

FACTSURFER

Factsurfer.com gives you a safe, fun way to find more information.

1. Go to www.factsurfer.com
2. Enter "Ligue 1" into the search box and click 🔍.
3. Select your book cover to see a list of related content.

INDEX

The images in this book are reproduced through the courtesy of: FEP via AP/ AP Images, cover; Action Plus Sports Images/ Alamy, p. 3; Sipa USA via AP/ AP Images, pp. 4, 4-5, 5 (top teams), 6, 11 (2023 Ligue 1 match, 2023), 12, 13; ASSOCIATED PRESS/ AP Images, p. 7; Skblzz1/ Wiki Commons, p. 8; Alain Gadoffre/ Getty Images, pp. 10 (2002 Ligue 1 match, 1995), 11 (2002); History and Art Collection/ Alamy, p. 10 (1932); PapaYves/ Wiki Commons, p. 10 (1933); Victor Joly/ Alamy, pp. 13 (here and there), 18; Sipa USA/ AP Images, p. 14; Independent Photo Agency/ Alamy, p. 16 (2024 Champions League Match); DPPI/ Alamy, pp. 17 (2023 Coupe de France match), 21 (Mickaël Landreau); Universal/ Getty Images, p. 19 (Raymond Kopa); Michel Barrault/ Getty Images, pp. 19 (Delio Onnis), 21 (Delio Onnis); ALLSTAR PICTURE LIBRARY/ Alamy, p. 19 (Jean-Pierre Papin); Neal Simpson/ Alamy, p. 19 (Zinedine Zidane); Cesar Ortiz Gonzalez/ Alamy, p. 19 (Kylian Mbappé); Orange Pictures/ Alamy, p. 20 (top); PhotoLondonUK, p. 20 (Orange Vélodrome); -/AFP/ Getty Images, p. 21 (Josip Skoblar); MB Media Solutions Ltd/ Alamy, p. 21 (Kylian Mbappé); Actionplus/ Alamy, p. 23.